AF593363

FOREWORD BY BISHOP DR. PRINCE HAMPEL

CRITICISM

How to Safeguard Your Heart Against Destructive Criticism

EBENEZER OSEI BONSU

LIVING WITH CRITICISMS

Design and Formatting: Nonon Tech & Design

ISBN: 978-9988-3-1833-8

Mother's Publishing™
We Care For Your Every Book Need

TABLE OF CONTENTS

COMMENT

The word criticism connotes a negative sentiment and we all hate to be criticized. But criticism is simply because we have different ways of seeing an issue. If we see criticism that way, then we can all benefit from it whether we classify it as constructive or destructive.

So, the first attitude that we must have to benefit from criticism is to develop an open mind and respect for other's opinion. Another important trait we must develop in order to benefit from criticism is Humility. The Bible warns us not to consider too highly of ourselves but to consider others as more important than ourselves (Philippians 2:4). It is only with this kind of attitude that we can benefit from the opinion expressed by another person, however opposed they may be from your own opinion.

The story is told of one, American President – Abraham Lincoln, that the commanding General of his armies described a decision he took as "foolish". The reply of the President was that, if the general says the decision was foolish, then he must be right, because he knows more about these issues than I do. This is an example of humility in a leader who respects the opinion of others.

To be successful in life, we also need to develop the art of critical thinking. This is where you learn to criticize yourself, or look at a wider perspective of the issue instead of focusing on the negative. A person who is a critical thinker always comes out with the best way of solving a problem.

In this book, what the author has sought to do is to draw our attention to the reality of criticism whether you describe it as constructive or destructive. He points out that, what is important is how you develop the right attitude in handling criticism. Every leader needs to develop this attitude. This book will contribute greatly to your understanding and how you handle criticism. I congratulate him for this piece of work and recommend it to you for your leadership development.

RT. REV. PROF. OSEI SAFO-KANTANKA

(Agricultural scientist, a former lecturer in plant breeding and Genetics and a former Bishop Of the Methodist Church Ghana)

FOREWORD

Nobody likes being criticized but unfortunately it is a fact of life. To be able to respond to criticism with nobility and detachment is an important life skill, which people have. If we respond to criticism without careful consideration, it can easily lead to unnecessary suffering.

Most criticism is probably based, at least in part, or on some truths. Criticism may appear negative. But through criticism we have the opportunity to learn and improve from their suggestions.

More and more, it seems like people want to grow, become great, but they don't want to be criticized. They need a shot in the arm, a call back to the virtue, ethics, morality, and importance of criticism. And that, folks, is why I love this book.

Living with criticism is about regular people. Whether you are successful in life, ministry, business or a big-time corporate leader, the author shows you a whole new mindset about life. He points out to the fact that, to be successful in life, we must never let people's compliments get to our head and their criticism get to our heart.

The author's uncanny insights and Holy Spirit led inspirations are so specific and easily applied, I believe they can empower any reader, regardless your background, to aspire to grow in the midst of criticism.

Bishop Dr. Prince Hampel
(Founder & President, Liberty Global Church / Minister Manna Int'l & Wisdom for Living)
Germany

ACKNOWLEDGEMENTS

To every great work there are great men and women who works behind the scenes to make things happen. It took the tireless effort of some great personalities for this wonderful work to come out handy.

I want to acknowledge Rev. Father Dr. Asante who gave me the needed motivation when I first had the inspiration from God to come out with a book. His words were so soothing that it gave me a different belief about myself. Also, to Elder Boakye, a lecturer at the University of Energy, who in spite of his busy schedule took time to edit the book for me. His mentoring and godly counsel over the years has actually reduced my burden in Ministry.

To my mothers, Dr Matilda Osei-Bonsu, Mama Benedicta Appiah and my biological Mum, Akua Afriyie, for making me who I am today. Also, to my good friends, Joel Adamu and Lawrence Abakisi, you guys are a blessing. How can I forget the encouragement from my Brothers, Kwabena Peprah and Edward Manu and all my other siblings. I can go on with the names without stopping but I'm limited by time. Everyone who has helped me in one way or the other, I want to say I'm eternally grateful. Everything you've done is greatly appreciated.

INTRODUCTION

"To avoid criticism say nothing, do nothing, be nothing."

- Elbert Hubbard

The famous people we celebrate today have had to learn how to live with criticisms. There is no way one will be great without going through criticisms. Any Greatness without criticism is a temporal greatness. Show me a person who is great and I will show you the number of criticisms he had to endure to get to where he has gotten to. The celebrities and the great men of influence we are modeling our lives after, have had to withstand some amount of criticisms in their bid to become great. Some of such criticisms were destructive while others were constructive.

The height we will attain in life is directly proportional to the number of criticisms that comes our way. One thing we must come to accept is that, people are entitled to their own opinions and no matter our actions towards them, they are still free to talk, either against us or in favor of us. The onus is on us to be ready to handle and live with every criticism that is directed to us whether bad or good. People try to be nice in order to avoid being criticized, but the truth is, ***there is no***

way one will do anything worthwhile in this world and avoid criticism. The only way to escape criticism is not to attempt doing anything worthwhile.

Many were the people who carried great visions and dreams, but criticisms trampled on them in their pursuit to discover who they were made to be. ***The graves are full of people who could not handle criticisms and chose rather to die than to be criticized. The road to greatness as discovered is criticism. Criticisms are bound to come no matter how nice we treat people.*** We can empty ourselves for people and yet be destructively criticized. We must go through life with the understanding that at every point in time we can meet people who will criticize even our good actions.

We know and have heard of lots of prominent people including Pastors, lawyers, doctors etc. who have given up on their professions and their God given callings because of criticisms. People who had the capacity to be Presidents, Mayors, Lecturers, and CEOs have giving up because of the negative words they heard from people they never expected it from. We do not expect all the people around us to make us happy, if we fail to create that atmosphere ourselves. ***We must learn to appreciate ourselves and expect nothing from anyone.*** If people compliment us, it should be a bonus and not a requirement else we will never be happy in life. This was what Jesus said,

"Woe unto you, when all men shall speak well of you! For so did their fathers to the false prophets"

Luke 6:26

This is a straightforward truth about life. Not everyone will appreciate you and not everyone will be happy even if you give him or her your very best. Building confidence in man and trusting that no man can hurt you is something we must never imagine. Those we even call family members and friends can be critical of us. It is usually said that the day we kill all our enemies we will have no friends around us. This means that majority of the people we call friends are not friends, but enemies in disguise. When we understand this simple truth, life will be more pleasant and we will not have to cry our heads off because of someone's opinion about us.

Get set for an empowerment as you go through the chapters of this book. It is my prayers that the illumination that comes as you go through the chapters will help you make the right decision no matter the opinion of people about you.

FORMS OF CRITICISMS

Constructive Criticism

Throughout our lives as individuals, we go through series of criticisms. There is no way someone can say he has avoided being criticized through all the stages of his or her life. Our parents, teachers, mentors among others through our formative years have criticized us in one way or the other and some of us are still open to such criticisms. Every good parent will make sure his child is instructed to take the right direction in life and in order to do that they shape us with scolding and what seems like a mild punishment or open rebuke just to put us to order. In schools we meet teachers who always criticize and challenge us to be better.

That is criticism, nonetheless in its constructive form. The criticisms we receive mostly from our parents, teachers, and mentors do not have the intentions to hurt but to make us trustworthy and responsible individuals. It is birthed out of genuine love and a greater desire to see us succeed.

"For whom the Lord loveth he chasteneth, and scourgeth every son whom he receiveth"

Hebrews 12,6

The purpose of parental criticism is not to destroy us, but to bring out the best in us. It is done constructively. Everyone who has been mentored before can testify to this fact. Mentors normally challenge us to do better through constant criticisms and open rebuke with no intention to destroy us. It is one of the many attributes of love, to chasten and scourge those we claim to love just as the Lord does with His loved ones. The word 'chasten' in the above scripture is translated 'paideuō' which means, to train, to be instructed or taught or learn or to chastise with words or to be corrected.

Destructive Criticism

The other criticism apart from the one intended to build the character of its victims is destructive criticism. Destructive criticism has no goal to demonstrate love or to put us on track. It is very destructive as the name goes.

The Collins dictionary defines it as the act or an instance of making an unfavorable or severe judgment, comment [to kill someone's self-esteem]. Others have also defined it as a criticism performed with the intention to harm someone, derogate and destroy someone's creation, prestige, reputation and self-esteem. Criticisms of this kind are very deadly and poisonous to the mind.

The Bible has several to say about destructive criticism. The Prophet Nehemiah was confronted with critics when he began to rebuild the walls of Jerusalem. Tobias and Sanballat as they were called came against the idea whiles they were making progress in building the walls. Their plan was to frustrate and discourage the builders and to do that they employed destructive criticism tactics. The verse three of the book of Nehemiah the chapter number four, gives us the comment they made about the wall.

"Now Tobiah the Ammonite was by him, and he said, even that which they build, if a fox goes up, he shall even break down their stone wall"

Nehemiah 4,3

What they said had the capacity to kill the interest of Nehemiah in helping his nation. A wall they had spent sleepless nights building and had wasted so much resources on, only to be told that a slight effort of a fox on it could easily knock it down.

Interestingly, this is how the Good News Bible puts their comment,

"What kind of wall could they ever build? Even a fox could knock it down!"

Perhaps you and I may be thinking they could be right with what they said. However, a careful study of the Bible portrays the opposite. The wall was not weak as they claimed. They said it on purpose to kill their interest to continue building the walls. The statement, what kind of wall could they ever build, ever emphasized, means nothing they built could be good enough. Destructive criticism is unfriendly and unfavorable and has the capacity to kill a person's interest of whatever he may be pursuing.

The Four Goals of Destructive Criticism

Mostly those who criticize us destructively may have a goal and intentions in doing that. I believe people don't just wake up and become critical of you, not without having a goal. The story of Nehemiah and his enemies as the Bible describes them, teaches us a lot. They had diabolic intentions that were not known to Nehemiah. Their plan was to frustrate them to give up building the walls.

We meet these critics in all our everyday endeavors. We meet them at the workplace, in the market, in schools among other places. Sometimes those we trust and call our friends may all have negative ulterior motives. We must therefore know the goals of the people who criticize us destructively and when we become aware of them, we will not be bothered because we are already aware of what they want to achieve with their words.

Let us look at the four general goals of every destructive criticism.

It Is Meant to Discourage

The reason why people mostly become critical of us even when we have done nothing to deserve that is to discourage us from whatever we are pursuing. The gift we carry and how unique we act many a times threaten those around us. At the workplace we can be confronted with strong hatred from people we might not necessarily know including our own colleagues. Such people begin to criticize us and find fault with everything we do. They do that on purpose to discourage us and in the process if we quit then they have achieved their goal.

Some people are good at discovering the potentials we carry inside of us that we ourselves may not even have any idea about. This automatically makes us a threat to whatever they may be enjoying including the positions they occupy and the little favors probably they may be getting. Destructive criticism becomes their last resort to make us give up.

The devil mostly incites people to criticize us especially when he discovers that we carry something that can be a threat to his kingdom.

I know people who had the potential of becoming great musicians but somewhere along the line they stopped pursuing that passion because someone told them "they had a horrible voice". This and many more of such destructive words are released with the purpose of discouraging us from pursuing what could bring blessings to us and the people around us.

I remember some years ago, in one of our church meetings, I was confronted by our Sunday school teacher whiles we were worshipping God in songs. All I heard was, "stop singing!" they all stopped and the leader walked up to me as everyone was watching. In what I presumed a very angry tone, she told me in front of everyone that I was distracting her with my voice. In short, what she meant was that my voice was horrible and that I should be quiet while those with good voices sang. I became so depressed and I nearly left church that day. I'm a great singer and so I saw that as an attempt by the devil to discourage me from going to church. We must know our worth before we allow someone to define us in a way we might not like. I overcame her words immediately I discovered that it was meant to discourage me. Her words could have put me off if I had not discovered that which know earlier. In church you will meet them. All we need to do is to never be discouraged by what others think of us. It could be the devil's attempt to deter us from pursuing the potential we carry inside of us. Imagine if I had given up church by listening to her words. I know I would not have gotten to where I am now. This is what one great thinker had to say, "Everywhere I go I'm asked if I think the university stifles writers. My opinion is that they don't stifle enough of them. There's many a best-seller that could have been prevented by a good teacher." (Flannery O'Connor). If care is not taken, we will allow ourselves to be prevented from pursuing our God given gift by the opinion of men. We must always be encouraged instead of getting discouraged because of the opinion of a mere mortal.

It Is Meant to Disgrace

Destructive criticisms come with so many branches and each one of the branches has the capacity to weaken any fragile heart. One other attempt of destructive criticism is to disgrace. Imagine when you are being berated in front of people you are shy of, or people who respect you, that "you are dull" or "empty headed" because of something you could not do. This might not sound too harsh for some people but the timing and where it was released can serve as the basis to ruin a person's entire happiness depending on the way he receives it. This is how some people will want to make you feel. They will always want to make you look useless and valueless in front of your friends and those who respect you. They do that on purpose to disgrace you so that you will give up on what might have scared them about you. A lot of folks have been disgraced by the words of others and as a result have given up on doing what they were supposed to do to be great.

You must try your best to Laugh at the negative words you hear about yourself instead of crying and worrying over it. Words meant to dis-grace has killed and weaken several individuals since they did not have the inner strength to deal and live with it. People will criticize us anyways so we better learn to face it no matter how bitter it may sound. Instead of making disgrace overpower us, we must be ready to overpower it. People can speak in ways that will always make us feel useless and worthless in front of our colleagues and playmates. We must build that inner strength and confidence to resist such destructive criticisms.

It Is Meant to Destroy

Several reputations have been soiled and tarnished by the words of the victims' haters. Some statements have been made to tag some pastor's evil and worldly, meanwhile they did nothing to deserve that. It is the attempt of this generation to destroy some hard-earned reputations of people who are on the road to achieve greater heights. People cannot withstand it when they see us prospering and making higher waves and not them. They will as a result resort to many evil ways to making sure we are destroyed. They will rain evil criticisms or negatively fueled words that we probably have no idea of just to defame us.

The instrument also of the churl are evil: he deviseth wicked devices to destroy the poor with lying words, even when the needy speak right.

Isaiah 32,7

Come and let us smite him with the tongue, and let us not give heed to any of his words.

Jeremiah 18,18b

The tongue of men has succeeded in destroying more lives than what chemical weapons and diseases have achieved. The human tongue is more deadly and unruly as Apostle James puts it in James 3:1-7. That is why we must guard our hearts against the negative words people release against us. Several lives have been destroyed because of the words that got hold of them. If our haters try all means necessary to destroy us and do not succeed, what they use are their words.

Never give anyone chance to ruin you by evil criticism. Your haters will always have a goal of destroying you more especially with their words. This was what the enemies of Prophet Jeremiah had to say "come and let us smite him with the tongue…" it is their tongue and not a sword or a gun. It is up to us then to decide whether we allow the evil tongue of others to destroy us or not to destroy us.

It Is Meant to Kill

Majority of suicide cases can be attributed to those who could not handle some words that were told them. A girl committed suicide and left this note for her parents "I'm useless as you have always said and I'm not fit to live". When people discover that you are weak at their words, they will stop at nothing but use it against you. They will say all kinds of things to make you feel you're not fit to live or be in a certain position. We should never kowtow instead we must rise up against their negative utterances.

It is an attempt by the devil to make us think and feel that we are not fit to live and he somehow incite the people around us to achieve this goal. Inside each and every one of us lies a bigger and a powerful dream yet to be unraveled that has the ability to bless the entire world.

I say this more passionately; never you see death as an option particularly because of someone's opinion about you. The devil's goal may be to kill us and ultimately kill that dream we carry inside of us that the world awaits earnestly for, with these words. Never you kill yourself.

Bill Gates, Dangote, Jack Ma and most of the influential individuals we hear of, have all been criticized destructively before, but the good news is that they never saw death as the first or last option, neither did they give up on their dreams. People's opinion about them did not change them to give up on what they were made to be. When people hate you, their words are strategically released to hurt you. Do not be bothered again of the kind of words you hear else it will have you killed if not physically, mentally. The decision is in our hands therefore to decide whether we allow ourselves to be killed by the words people release against us.

These are the four goals of the people who destructively criticize us. Now that we are aware of them, never must we fret ourselves again when someone criticizes us wrongly. However, we must be encouraged since we now know what they want to achieve with their words.

WHY PEOPLE CRITICIZE DESTRUCTIVELY

It will be abject denial on our part to think we must necessarily sin against someone before they can in turn have the ticket to speak evil of us. Normally we hear some folks cry "what did I do wrong to deserve all that?" ***The fact of the matter is that you do not have to wrong someone before they hate you. Criticisms can be directed towards us from all angles including people we have never even met before, so long as what we do serves as an offence to them.*** Someone might hate you the very first time he crosses your path for reasons you might never know and understand. Such is life and we must understand and embrace it.

With my few years in the ministry, I have discovered some three basic reasons why preachers, friends, bosses, colleagues etc. will destructively criticize one another or their subordinates. It is so common in our days to hear businesses berating other businesses; journalists tongue-lashing their fellow journalists; preachers of the gospel castigating other men of God. Why will they do that? In our churches and work places, we experience several of such cases.

The three reasons as I have discovered are: fear, envy and insecurity. There may be more, nevertheless these are the major reasons why someone will destructively criticize you to bring your hard-earned reputation and some potential we may carry into destruction.

FEAR

The dread of us most of the times incites people to harshly criticize us. ***Our presence alone and sometimes some unique qualities we possess can scare the hell out of people.*** They will develop strong hatred for us that manifests in the way they talk to us. This may be a low blow but let's take for instance, having master's degree and working with a superior whose qualification is merely a diploma. The fear for his job can inconsiderably cause a wedge or hatred coupled with criticisms against you even when you seem to present brilliant ideas. It may not be because you will eventually offend him but because of his fear that you can be given his position at any given opportunity. Trust me, he will find reasons to undermine you and will always criticize you for trivial matters, you might never understand. There is nothing you will do that will be appreciated by him.

Allow me to reiterate, some people have eyes to spot great potentials and discern what our future may look like. It could probably be in the way we conduct ourselves, the way we speak and our dedication towards work. This generates fear in the heart of the people around us especially when they see us to be a competition to whatever favors they may be enjoying.

The children of Israel in their wilderness journey came into close contact with several oppositions from different nations. The Israelites never insulted any nation or touched anything belonging to any nation but they were confronted with different attacks from all angles because of their very essence. Great nations were in fear at their presence and tried all means necessary to eliminate or avoid them.

"And Moab was sore afraid of the people, because they were many: and Moab was distressed because of the children of Israel"

Numbers 22:4

The Moabites' hatred for Israel was not as a result of what the Israelites did against them. As a matter of fact, the Israelites were just passing through to their promised land and somehow came across the Moabites. They were greatly afraid because of the news they had heard about the children of Israel, the wealth they carried and how nations had been conquered by them. The Moabite's fear made them to go and get the service of an old Prophet to curse them.

I want you to note something here, just the presence of the children of Israel startled the Moabites. ***People will criticize you wrongly not because of what you have done against them but because of something unique you possess that serves as a threat to them.*** We hear pastors criticizing their fellow pastors, managing directors, musicians among others and we normally cannot figure out the reasons. Mostly it comes as a result of fear. Those they criticize may be posing as a threat or a competition to whatever they may be enjoying. When people wrongly criticize you from today forward, do not be bothered rather persevere. It could be that they have discovered something extraordinary about you that they are very much afraid of.

"And Saul was very wroth, and the saying displeased him; and he said, they have ascribed unto David ten thousand, and to me they have ascribed but thousands: and what can he have more but the kingdom?"

1Samuel 18:8

King Saul's hatred for David as we are aware, was not because the young David killed a man he could not kill, being the leader and peradventure the commander in chief of the armies of Israel. He could live with David killing Goliath but he simply could not live with the song he heard the women sing. The women after the war came out jubilating and dancing and the song they were singing was "Saul hath slain his thousands, and David his ten thousand" Saul hearing this song from the women developed a strong fear and hatred for David because of fear of losing the throne and his kingdom to him. He became so afraid from that day and wanted to kill David. He saw him as a competition.

"And Saul cast the javelin; for he said, I will smite David even to the wall with it. And David avoided out of his presence twice"

1 Samuel 18:11

Saul's fear that David was going to take the kingdom from his hands made him cast a javelin to destroy him. ***The truth is that people will not stop casting javelins from their mouths to destroy you as long as you remain a threat to them,*** but like David, we must avoid their presence. You must learn how to resist the words of people whose goal is to destroy you.

Envy

Majority of the criticisms we face comes as a result of envy. ***The day we decide to do things differently from others, they become envious of us. Living an enviable life brings criticisms of all kinds.*** People will try all they can to stop you with their words. Words like “he is arrogant”, “he thinks he has arrived”, “he has gone for juju or he is fetish” “we will live to see” and such likes, will be so common to your hearing. These are mostly words of envy. Envy is most evident among peers, classmates, colleagues and people of the same social strata. You appear to be at the same level until you feel the need for change and then you become an automatic target for envy.

Change is very difficult for most individuals and so any time one decides to change the status quo and move on the ladder of change makers several criticisms will come against him.

“When Sanballat the Horonite, and Tobiah the servant, the Ammonite, heard of it, it grieved them exceedingly that there was come a man to seek the welfare of the children of Israel”

Nehemiah 2:10

The Israelites became vulnerable to enemy attack when their walls broke down. For years they had no one to come to their aid but eventually God touched Nehemiah’s heart and he drove all the way from the palace of Shushan where he was serving as a king's cupbearer. He came with all the materials needed for the rebuilding of the wall. As we read, Sanballat and Tobiah became aggrieved for the mere reason that someone had come from a far to seek the welfare of the children of Israel. For all we know they were Nehemiah's age mate and they were thinking in their heart that he thinks he is better than us. This was envy in operation. Left to them the Israelites should remained vulnerable for the rest of their lives than allow someone who had not been with them to come and build the city wall. That is how it is in life, the day we begin to make giant strides in whichever career we have chosen to pursue and we begin to show signs of prosperity and victory, people will be envious and as a result attack us to make us give up.

Some will falsely criticize us of the things we know nothing about. Every level we get to in this life, remember, we will meet our Tobiah and Sanballat. This was what they said out of envy to Nehemiah.

"Now Tobiah the Ammonite was by him, and he said, even that which they build, if a fox goes up, He shall even break down their stone wall"

Nehemiah 4:3

Out of envy people will find fault with anything we do more especially when they discover that our chances of success and winning are higher. Mark Zuckerberg, the owner of Facebook, in his speech at Harvard said, he was confronted with several criticisms when he began the idea of Facebook. As he explained, all his counterparts eventually left him. "While I had a vision of connecting the world, others were not in agreement" he said. People became envious when he started gaining popularity. He said and I quote "an advisor told me if I did not agree to sell, I would regret the decision for the rest of my life. Relationship were so frayed that within a year or so every single person on the management team was gone."

We must endeavor to see destructive criticism as a normal phenomenon that has become part and parcel of our world, unless of course we do not want to make any meaningful impact that will bring about progress and success. Imagine if Mark Zuckerberg had given up all because of back lash, what would have happened? The world would have missed on this global connection that's so important today.

INSECURITY

"When people say bad things about you it's only because they are insecure. So next time when someone says something mean, remember, it has nothing to do with you but everything to do with them" (Anonymous).

Beside fear and envy, people tend to criticize mostly because of the lack of self-confidence in themselves. They do everything possible to criticize wrongly either to bring people to their level or to appear confident. They do not have the confidence to try their hands on enough things and so when they see people who have the ability to do that, it threatens them and they resort to criticisms. They see people who possess what they lack as a danger around them. In order to eradicate such people from their lives, they insult, mistreat and criticize them. People who live in insecurity would not take it lightly when they see you as a competition. Appreciating people is never in their genes because of their lack of confidence in themselves. Expecting praises from someone who is insecure is like expecting darkness to overcome light which is rightly impossible. This is the reason why we must not be perturbed when people destructively criticize us. The fault they find with us have nothing to do with us but everything to do with them.

BENEFITS OF CRITICISM

Handling Criticism comes to us like the pen we use to write. One can decide to use it to write encouraging words, messages of hope or decide to use it to write songs. Others can also decide to use it to write fake cheques and for other evil purposes. It is the same pen but its usage depends on the one who has it in his possession. The destructive words that come against us can either be used to build ourselves up or allow ourselves to be ruined by it. ***No one can imprison our minds without our consent.*** The choice is ours to make. Destructive criticism can come with so many benefits when one has learnt the various ways of handling it. In this chapter we are going to look at some benefits that can be carved out of a destructive criticism.

It Brings Improvement

Depending on how we look at it, criticisms can help us to improve. Metaphorically speaking, when someone hauls a stone at you, it's your choice to either swerve, grabbing it and using it as a stepping stone to another level or you can allow yourself to be hit and hurt by it, destroying you in the process. ***We must endeavor to see opportunity in every destructive utterance people hurl at us.*** A lot of people out of the barrels of criticisms they have received have been able to work on themselves to be better people, although the intentions of the criticism that was thrown at them were evil. The honest truth is that some of the criticisms challenge us to work harder on ourselves even if its intent is to harm us. Instead of letting the harsh words released against us destroy us, we can use it to improve upon ourselves.

In the Bible, Hannah the mother of Prophet Samuel was criticized and mocked by her rival because she was barren. If it were to be some of us, we would have given up on ourselves by leaving the marriage or worse considering suicide. However, Hannah instead of doing any chose rather to be provoked to intensify her prayers which eventually made God to answer her request. The provocation of the rival, although was evil actually pushed Hannah to be fervent and effectual in her prayers.

"And her adversary also provoked her sore for to make her fret, because the Lord had shut up her womb. And she was in bitterness of soul, and prayed unto the LORD, and wept sore"

1 Samuel 1:6 & 10

Hannah used the criticism and mockery of her rival to her advantage and became prayerful. Although the intention of the rival was to make her fret, Hannah had her breakthrough out of that.

It Gives Us A Cue of The Path Chosen in Life

There is no way you will do anything worthwhile and not be criticized. ***Remember this, immediately you step your foot on the path of greatness, criticism will meet and welcome you.*** The day you decide to do something new that people are not familiar with, they will rise up and criticize you in order to make you quit. The human society is generally anti-change. We always want to maintain the status quo and do things conventionally and so anytime one decides to introduce something that is not in line with our old ways of doing things, it incurs wrath. But as I have come to understand, ***anytime you start something and you face severe criticism that makes you want to give up, it's mostly a cue that you are on the right path.*** Time will not permit me to tell you about people who withstood destructive criticism and amazingly the very thing they were criticized for, lifted them to a place of prominence when they relented not. ***Anytime people try to obstruct you with their words purposefully just to make you give up on something good you have started, remember to push further because you might not know but you may be up to something great.***

David's next level to become a king was at the battlefield where Goliath was defiling the armies of the God of Israel. Killing Goliath, the giant of all time who made a whole army to run for their lives, was going to be the beginning of David's kingship. The opposite could have also been true. David was however confronted with a great criticism when he decided to face what could make him a King. The Bible records, one of his brothers undermined David with his words and with the aim of discouraging him to give up the idea of fighting the Giant.

"And Eliab his eldest brother heard when he spake unto the men; and Eliab's anger was kindled against David. And he said why, why camest thou down hither? And with whom hast thou left those few sheep in the wilderness? I know thy pride and the naughtiness of thine heart; for thou art come down that thou mightiest see the battle"

1 Samuel 17:28

David was set for a breakthrough but a great confrontation came from his brothers. That did not cause him to give up. David saw the criticism raised against him as a cue for his breakthrough. ***David had learnt that, behind every bad confrontation there is always a promotion.*** He was never moved to give up. His brother said "I know thy pride and the naughtiness of thine heart". This criticism was enough to have caused David to give up, but it did not, he realized his next level was due and that was the reason for the criticism.

It Can Be A Stepping Stone To Turn Our Weaknesses into Strength

Destructive criticism sometimes may be the truth spoken in a wrong way. It could be true that people who are critical about us may be speaking the truth however employing a wrong way of sending the message across. Therefore, it will be mostly prudent on our part to give ourselves time and space to examine the criticism, if there be any truth to it. That is not to say we must allow ourselves to be eaten up by the criticism. For instance, if someone calls a book you have spent months writing "pure rubbish" or someone calls you "arrogant", it is destructive indeed but you can do an extra check to see whether what they have said is true. There may be a bit of truth in the criticism but spoken in a way that can make you give up. Just give yourself sometime and do a personal check of your own life to see whether there are flaws as you have been described. Whether truly you are showing signs of arrogance or not.

But as for you, ye thought evil against me; But God meant it unto good...

Genesis 50:20

The aim of releasing a destructive word may be negative but we can use it to work on ourselves. Joseph in the scripture above was sold into slavery to die but instead of dying, he took time to prepare himself in and out of service and became a prime minister, nonetheless through the same evil act of his brothers. His brother's motive for selling him was wrong and deadly but eventually it turned out to be something good.

That is exactly what I mean by saying take time to reflect on some criticisms people release against you just so to work on yourself. The intentions of the criticism may be to harm and disgrace you but you can reflect on it and pick the little truth it may carry or take some lessons out of it. If someone comes hurling insults and criticisms at you, learn to ignore it, and extract substance if it has any but if not, just forget it. Selling Joseph out is just like the destructive criticism people release. The intention may be evil but it can later be positive if we learn to absorb the little truth it may carry to work on ourselves.

JESUS, OUR PERFECT ROLE MODEL

No human person has ever been criticized in the History of mankind than Jesus Christ, the true Son of God. He was the promised Messiah. All the Prophets of old spoke about him even from His birth up till the time He began His ministry. He suffered many things in the hands of cruel men but none of those things moved Him to give up on His assignment. He firmly stood His grounds because He knew all men and did not commit himself unto them (John 2, 24). This makes him our perfect role model in suffering and in criticism. Any suffering we think we are undergoing; Jesus went through it first and yet never sinned nor gave up.

For we have not an high priest which cannot be touched with the feeling of our infirmities; but was in all points tempted like as we are, yet without sin.

Hebrews 4:15

The evil words of men we hear in our ears always, He encountered worst of them and has become a perfect example for us in all things.

"For even hereunto were ye called: because Christ also suffered for us, leaving us an example, that ye should follow his steps: who did no sin, neither was guile found in his mouth: who, when he was reviled, reviled not again; when he suffered, he threatened not; but committed himself to him that judgeth righteously..."

1 Peter 2:21-23

Jesus Christ suffered various degrees of criticisms from all angles but none of those deterred him from His purpose. He overcame all that was said about Him as He set his gaze on the assignment His Father commissioned him to do. He was "reviled" as the Bible records, which means He was attacked with abusive language and yet that could not overcome Him. In the next chapter I will give you ways we can overcome the abusive words of men. Let us now look at the various angles Jesus was criticized throughout his earthly life and ministry.

What People Criticized of Jesus:

His Good Deeds

The day we decide to do things differently from what people already know, that will be the day we will vehemently be opposed. Jesus in his earthly ministry came to set a different path from what people were already familiar with and accustomed to. There were so many religious sects including the Pharisees, Sadducees, the Scribes among others, but Jesus made it a point to be different because of his assignment.

> *And they were astonished at his doctrine: for he taught them as one that had authority, and not as the scribes*
>
> *Mark 1:22*

He did things differently from what the people around him had grown up to embrace. The society He was born into, had a strong believe with regards to the Sabbath. To them the sacredness of the Sabbath was everything and any breach of it was tantamount to stoning. If someone was even at the point of death and unfortunately for the person it falls on the Sabbath day, no hospital or physician had the power to attend to such a person. That was the level the Sabbath took and the level they were willing to go. Jesus growing up realized that the intents of the Sabbath was misunderstood among His people. Instead of bringing happiness, the Sabbath was rather restricting the happiness of men. He then made it a point to teach men the essence of the Sabbath by ministering healing to everyone who called for help regardless of the day. This brought great hatred from every side against him. ***Criticisms of all kinds were rained on him to cause him to give up on His good deeds especially on the Sabbath day.*** Listen, *people will rain criticism the day you decide to change a trend or a long-standing tradition.* To them good deeds had a limit when it falls on the Sabbath day. That was the trend and the tradition they had followed all their lives but Jesus had it all different and proved beyond reasonable doubts that good deeds had no limit. The issue is that people will not take it lightly when you decide to break free from limitations that might have slowed everyone down. Verbal abuse of all kinds will be raised against you. They will tell you; you have -gone for "juju" or the latest criticism "you are arrogant" among other detractions just because you chose to do things in your own unique way.

All Jesus' good deeds were misunderstood by men and as such received their anger because he found himself in a society where such things were not common. Jesus at a point questioned them on the issue of the Sabbath because of the several criticisms He was receiving.

"And he saith unto them, is it lawful to do good on the Sabbath days, or to do evil? To save life, or to kill? But they held their peace"

Mark 3:4

"And the ruler of the synagogue answered with indignation, because that Jesus had healed on the Sabbath day, and said unto the people, there are six days in which men ought to work: in them therefore come and be healed, and not on the Sabbath day. The Lord then answered him, and said, thou hypocrite, doth not each one of you on the Sabbath lose his ox or his ass from the stall, and lead him away to watering? And ought not this woman, being a daughter of Abraham, whom Satan hath bound, lo, these eighteen years, be loosed from this bond on the Sabbath day? And when he said these things, all his adversaries were ashamed: and all the people rejoiced for all the glorious things that were done by him

Luke 13:15-17

In spite of all the good things he did for mankind, he was misunderstood and was criticized when he decided to change what was already known.

His Source of Power

People doubted the credibility of Jesus' ministry right from the beginning, including his own family. He did things that were not common to their minds. The family and the society he grew up saw him to be a threat to their peace. However, they did not know He was the King of peace. They criticized and criticized even his source of power. They saw him to be someone possessed and driven by demons because of the unusual miracles he performed.

"He came unto his own, and his own received him not"

John 1:11

They did not receive him because of how differently he chose to do things which was not the same as the already set standard. Friends criticized and forsook him; Family rejected him.

They had grown with the mentality that every sickness and infirmity required a Doctor and that it was never possible to live without sickness and be free from demonic oppression. This was the nature of the society Jesus grew up to meet. There were sick people everywhere. Demon possessed among others, even in their church meetings. People had even forgotten that healing was still possible. Jesus started his ministry performing miracles and healing everyone who was sick and oppressed by the devil. He came to set the records straight; man was not created to live a weak life under the bondage of sin. He healed sicknesses without any sweat. ***Strange diseases Doctors could not even understand gave way at Jesus' voice.*** The touch of His garment brought healing to the woman who had issue of blood for twelve good years. (Mark 5:25-29). He turned water into wine which was never done before. (John 2:7). Dead bodies came back to life at his voice. (John 11:43).

All these and several others were done by him and because it was not in line with their set standards, they started criticizing him.

When the Pharisees heard it, they said, this fellow doth not cast out devils, but by Beelzebub the prince of devils.

Matthew 12:24

And when he was come into the temple, the chief priests and the elders of the people came unto him as he was teaching, and said, by what authority doest thou these things? And who gave thee this authority."

Matthew 21:23

People never understood him and so they concluded he was using the spirit of Beelzebub, the prince of demons. Different forms of criticisms were levelled against him but none of those moved him since he was determined to bring about change. He was tagged demon possessed for his source of power but that did not stop our Lord Jesus.

His Relationship with People

How Jesus related with the people of his time brought several abusive criticisms. ***Jesus understood that, the best way he could win the weak was to identify himself with them and see Himself a part of them.*** This made him spend quality time with the notorious sinners of his time. He dined, played and laughed with them. The Pharisees seeing it misinterpreted his actions and saw him to be an imposter and a false teacher because they did not understand how someone who claimed to be the son of God could mingle with sinners (Matthew 9: 11). This did not move Jesus. We must ***never give people access into our lives to control what makes us happy more especially when we know it is in line with our assignment.*** They called Jesus different defamatory names and yet he was determined to make a mark. Remember, anything you do in this life will bring criticism. Even if you choose not do anything people will still criticize you. This was what Jesus said:

For john the Baptist came neither eating bread nor drinking wine; and ye say, he hath a devil. The Son of man is come eating and drinking; and ye say, behold a gluttonous man, and a winebibber, a friend of publicans and sinners!

Luke 7:33-34

The Pharisees expected Jesus to be walking with certain class of people and not sinners and publicans. That was the more reason why they doubted His Ministry and assignment. They were however ignorant of the fact that Jesus was setting a new path of righteousness which was entirely different from their crafted righteousness. The greatest commandment Jesus said was *"thou shalt love the Lord thy God with all thy heart, and with all thy soul, and with all thy mind. This is the first and great commandment. And the second is like unto it, thou shalt love thy neighbor as thyself"* (Matthew 22, 37-40). Jesus loved everyone like himself and so he demonstrated love to each and every one regardless of the person's state of mind. The Pharisees had it all wrong because they believed that righteousness was by the association one kept and not loving others as Jesus taught.

Jesus became a way maker for us the end time believers. He did things according to his mandate and not according to dictates of people. Every step he took was criticized but he was never discouraged. We must be determined to do new things to make news by not following the masses.

His Divinity

Everything about Jesus pointed at His identity as the true Son of God. From His miraculous birth and the happenings that preceded His birth. Even long before He began His mission, God sent a forerunner, in the person of John the Baptist who came ahead of time to announce to the world the nature of man He was to be. (John 1: 15) Many infallible proofs occurred at His birth and death which the Doctors of the law were aware of and had read about it from the scrolls, yet the opinion of the masses and their self-styled righteousness prevented them from believing. The signs, wonders and miracles that followed him wherever He went was supposed to have convinced them of His Divinity.

This was what Cornelius, a Pharisee and a ruler of the Jews said

"Rabbi, we know that thou art a teacher come from God: for no man can do these miracles that thou doest, except God be with him"

John 3:2

They knew very well that He was from God but they chose not to come out openly to declare their stand. People still criticized and doubted His Divinity.

"And when he was come into his own country, he taught them in their synagogue, insomuch that they were astonished, and said, whence hath this man this wisdom, and these mighty works? Is not this the carpenter's son? Is not his mother called Mary? And his brethren, James, and Joses and Simon, and Judas? And his sisters, are they not all with us? Whence then hath this man all these things."

Matthew 13:54-56

Jesus encountered several criticisms from His own people. They saw him to be a mere carpenter's Son and not the Messiah. Despite the many infallible proofs, they witnessed themselves, they still chose not to believe Him. Their unbelief coupled with criticisms could not make Him perform any miracle amongst them:

"But Jesus said to them, a prophet is not without honor, save in his own country, and in his own house. And he did not many mighty works there because of their unbelief"

Matthew 13:57-58

This is how many will try to undermine you the day you decide to be unique. We must get this, the fact that we are from the same family, taught by the same teacher and perhaps ate together, does not mean we have the same destiny. This mentality was what prevented the Jews from believing in Jesus' Divinity and as result criticized him. They taught he was one of them since He grew up among them. They criticized and insulted Him any time He demonstrated to them that He was from above. (John 8:57-59) For this reason they never benefited from His earthly ministry.

Jesus could have been stopped by the many criticisms that was raised against Him but he chose not to be controlled by any of them. He realized they were all opinions of mortals. He set His gaze on the one that sent him and committed himself fully into his care.

This teaches us that we have upper hand over all the things that happens around us. No man has control or mastery to influence our thinking unless we have given them the chance to do so. We can choose to overcome or be overcome by the opinions of men. Either way, it is your choice.

Destructive criticisms can be very deadly if we have not learnt how to handle and live with them. In the next chapter we are going to be looking at the various ways we can handle the sting of destructive criticisms.

HOW TO HANDLE DESTRUCTIVE CRITICISMS

Those who have learnt the various ways of handling destructive criticisms are the very ones who are making impact in our generation. It is often said that whether we act or do not act we will be criticized. Then as people determined to make an impact, we must act to be criticized than to be quiet and be criticized. There should be that readiness in our heart to deal with every criticism that comes to our way.

Over the years I have come across four basic ways that can help us handle criticisms that are meant to destroy and make life unbearable for us. We must take a critical look at them to safeguard our hearts from the destructive words of men.

Below are the four basic ways to destroy the sting of destructive criticism.

Selectively Choose the Words You Allow into Your Ears

"And he said unto them, take heed what ye hear..."

Mark 4:24

The human body is such that whatever we allow to enter our system has the potency to make or unmake us. The words we allow into our ears can corrupt our whole being. That is why the Bible warns that "evil communication corrupts good manners" (1 Cor. 15: 33). The evil criticisms people release against us, if allowed into our ears can corrupt our dreams and some hidden treasures God has put inside of us. We must consciously be selective of the kind of words we allow into our ears. The kind of words we allow into our ears can ruin us or make us reign in life. We must choose our words wisely and ***go to places where we will hear soul-lifting and constructive words and not destructive ones.*** There are people any time we go closer to them, they want to make us feel worthless and unimportant with their criticisms. Such people must be avoided because we become what we constantly listen to.

Jesus' foremost strategy he used to destroy the sting of poisonous criticisms was to shut his ears against destructive words. The day you open your ears to listen to destructive opinions of people concerning your life, trust me your life will be in danger. Jesus was criticized on every side he turned to, but he was so careful not to allow any of those words to enter into his ears to control his life.

Just as no one forces you to eat something you don't like; in the same way you can reject every word you don't like. You are the master of your own life and nobody alive or dead can control you, until you have given them access to do that.

Bishop Oyedepo in one of his messages said he received a letter in his office and when he discovered the source of the letter, he wrote at the back of the letter "Never to be read". He never touched the letter again until it was thrown into the trash can. I believe you are wondering why he did that. He said, he knew the person who wrote the letter and what the content was going to be like. "If I had read, it would have impacted my life negatively" he said.

There is some information we must never permit into our life. Information they say either brings deformation or transformation. The power is in our hands to choose what it offers us. We must train our ears to reject any destructive criticism. There are some words when we give heed to, it can dump our spiritual growth and kill every good seed we may carry inside of us. Jesus being our perfect example in criticism is warning us to "take heed what we hear" (Mark 4:24). Knowing what the things we hear can do to us.

Never Respond to Your Critics

Another powerful strategy Jesus employed to overcome the negative opinions of men against his life and ministry was the fact that he never responded to his critics. The more we try to explain ourselves to the people who destructively criticize us, the more we give them the power to keep on with their words. ***Responding to our enemies and the people who are critical about us, is like throwing ourselves into the pit someone has dug for us.*** Remember this song "he that is down needs fear no fall", it simply means the people who criticize us stands to lose nothing with our response because they are already down. We maintain our position at the top when we decide not to utter a word in response to people's opinion about us, else we drop ourselves down to their level. Every word we hear about ourselves that we think can serve as a stumbling block must be treated as "unheard". Keeping mute will leave our critics in total confusion because they cannot be sure whether we hear them or not. This was said about Jesus,

"He was oppressed, and he was afflicted, yet he opened not his mouth..."

Isaiah 53:7

Nothing disarms the enemies against our progress than our silence. Our silence is golden in matters of criticism. Jesus was oppressed and afflicted by the words of men, yet he never uttered anything because their words meant nothing to him.

"Then said Pilate unto him, hearest thou not how many things they witness against thee? And he answered him never a word; insomuch that the governor marveled greatly"

Matthew 27:13-14

As I said earlier on, we can give people all that we have as a gift and still be criticized. People are entitled to their own opinion, no matter our good deeds. Jesus the Messiah showed people so much kindness but they still did not cease talking against him. There was no need for him to respond to the criticisms and accusations they raised against him because they were going to talk anyways. The more we respond to the harsh criticisms people throw at us, the more we bring attention to them. Truth has a way of vindicating itself. Do not respond!! Over the years those who spent time responding to their critics ended up becoming like them.

"Who did no sin, neither was guile found in his mouth: who, when he was reviled, reviled not again; when he suffered, he threatened not; but committed himself to him that judgeth righteously..."

1 Peter 2:23

The most painful thing our enemies cannot handle is when we shut our mouth in defense without uttering a word against their criticisms. It makes them feel valueless and useless, however if we keep on spending our precious time responding to every criticism, we hear we make them feel important.

Consider Jesus Christ

In times of criticism we should always remember that we are followers of Jesus Christ. As a matter of fact, He is our Master. No servant is better than his master. As I indicated, Jesus faced severe criticisms even to the extent that they wanted to kill him before his time, yet he never gave in to their criticisms. He stood his grounds and accomplished his mission on earth.

"For even hereunto were ye called: because Christ also suffered for us, leaving us an example, that ye should follow his steps: who did no sin, neither was guile found in his mouth: who, when he was reviled, reviled not again; when he suffered, he threatened not; but committed himself to him that judgeth righteously..."

1 Peter 2, 21-23

All that he went through was to give us an example that we will have similar encounters, but just as he overcame, we can also overcome. We are not better than him and we can never be better than him and so as followers, we must remember that what he endured we will be confronted with similar attacks and we must also endure. This was Jesus' words to all his followers,

"Remember the word that I said unto you, the servant is not greater than his Lord. If they have persecuted me, they will also persecute you; if they have kept my saying they will keep yours also"

John 15:20

When people are criticizing you and you feel like giving up, remember Jesus Christ went through similar criticisms and overcame and so you too can overcome.

Making the Word of God Our Source of Hope

The word of God in us builds resistance which helps us to deal with circumstances beyond our control. The Word of God is a firm foundation everyone must rely on to deal with the evil words of men. People might have written you off, thinking nothing good will come out of your situation, but the Word of God is full of living testimonies of people who were criticized, marooned and were tagged valueless. Sarah, Elizabeth, Ruth, Jabez, Japhter and many others were all living in hopeless situations but God came in and turned their mourning into dancing. They trusted Him to be a faithful judge. The word in us ignites our hope that no matter the opinion of others about us we will one day be somebody.

"But God hath chosen the foolish things of the world to confound the wise; and God hath chosen the weak things of the world to confound things which are mighty; and base things of the world, and things which are not, to bring to nought things that are: that no flesh should glory in his presence."

1 Corinthians 1:27-29

Only the word of God can build that hope in us. "…Christ in you, the hope of glory" (Colossians 1:27). The Word is Christ and so having him inside of us, gives us a better hope of glory. This was what Paul told the believers he encountered before his death,

"And now, brethren, I commend you to God, and to the word of his grace, which is able to build you up, and give an inheritance among all them which are sanctified"

Acts 20:32

It is only the word of God which has the potency to build us up in all situations and nothing else. The reason why some people will choose death over life when they are badly criticized is because they do not have the word of God inside of them. Any least thing that happens to them, they conclude that their lives have come to an end.

The things we go through as believers are not different from what the unbelievers go through, but we overcome because of the Word of God inside of us. Sometimes when you hear what made someone commit suicide, you just cannot help but laugh and thank God for the life you still have. You realize you have gone through that series of times and yet you are alive. The word of God inside of us is the secret. It causes us to triumph in all situations. Nothing builds resistance in us more than the word of God.

I have just shared with you the mind of God. We must avoid crying and worrying over what someone thinks about us. Criticisms are inevitable but it is our singular responsibility and assignment to shield and safeguard our hearts against them. Going forward we must walk and have a definition for ourselves. Any additional definition in the form of destructive criticism must be rejected and trampled underfoot. People are entitled to their own opinion and you cannot change that. The only person you can change in this world is yourself and not anyone.

A Prayer for Salvation

God loves you- no matter who you are and what has happened in your past. He loves you so much that He sent His only begotten Son to die for you on the cross. Jesus Christ laid down his life and rose again so that "whosoever believes in Him would not perish but have everlasting life. God has been waiting for you all these years and His arms are rightly opened to receive you. If you would like to receive Jesus Christ into your life as your Lord and personal savior, say the following prayer out loud and mean it from your heart:

Heavenly Father, I come to You admitting that I am a sinner. Right now, I choose to turn away from sin, and I ask You to cleanse me of all unrighteousness. I believe that Your Son, Jesus, died on the cross to take away my sins. I also believe that He rose again from the dead so that I might be forgiven of my sins and made righteous through faith in Him. I call upon the name of Jesus Christ to be the Savior and Lord of my life. Jesus, I choose to follow You and ask that You fill me with the power of the Holy Spirit. I declare that right now I am a child of God. I am free from sin and full of the righteousness of God. I am saved in Jesus' name. Amen

If you have sincerely prayed this prayer, you have invited Jesus Christ into your life. Now, God is your Father and he hears you when you speak to Him in prayer. Find a bible believing church as your local assembly where you can join other body of believers to continue in Word, prayer and in fellowship for your spiritual growth. You can also contact us with the details on the last page:

About the Author

Ebenezer Osei Bonsu is a prolific writer, a passionate worship leader and a counselor. He obtained a bachelor's degree in Development Education Studies at the University for Development Studies and holds Masters in Theology at the Evergreen Bible College. He serves the body of Christ with his special prophetic and healing grace.

He is the founder of the Students Christian Fellowship on the University campus, a vibrant fellowship that has grown to train several leaders for Ministry. While studying at the University, he was awarded the most influential Student for his extraordinary service towards people of all class.

As a servant leader, he understands where people are and reaches out to them. He is a voice in this generation that encourages, informs and comforts men and women with godly counsel.

CONTACT THE AUTHOR

Mob: +233 205 569 679 / +233 244 849 817

Email: higherheight4@gmail.com

www.ingramcontent.com/pod-product-compliance
Lightning Source LLC
LaVergne TN
LVHW010502160826
845677LV00012B/2610

* 9 7 8 9 9 8 8 3 1 8 3 3 8 *